The Ages
In Tension

John V. Halvorson

Augsburg Publishing House
MINNEAPOLIS, MINNESOTA

THE AGES IN TENSION

Copyright © 1970 Augsburg Publishing House

All rights reserved

Library of Congress Catalog Card No. 70-121964

MANUFACTURED IN THE UNITED STATES OF AMERICA

To Hazel
and the children whom God has
given us

Acknowledgements

I wish to acknowledge my debt to several people: to my college teacher Dr. O. W. Qualley, Luther College, Decorah, Iowa, from whom I learned the need for thorough preparation; to my colleagues and the students of Luther Theological Seminary; to Paul Holmer, Yale University; to William F. Albright, Johns Hopkins University; to John Bright, Union Theological Seminary in Virginia; and to Reinhold Niebuhr, my teacher through the medium of books, articles and correspondence.

Contents

Foreword

by

Dr. John Bright

Union Theological Seminary

Richmond, Virginia

It is a pleasure to have this study from the pen of Professor Halvorson, for few concepts are of more central importance for the understanding of the Bible, and of the nature of the Christian's life within this world, than that of the two ages or aeons. This is especially true of the New Testament, where the concept plays such a dominant role. It is perhaps given its clearest formal expression by Paul in Romans 5 when he places Adam and Christ over against one another as type to antitype, and declares that as through the one man Adam sin and death entered the world, so through the one man Jesus Christ has come the free gift of righteousness and eternal life. Though he does not here use the expression, Paul clearly sees the whole of history as divided into two ages: the old age which began with Adam, and the new age inaugurated by Jesus Christ, who is the second Adam.

To be sure, explicit mention of the two ages is much less frequent, even in the New Testament, than one might expect. But the concept is far more pervasive than such an observation might lead one to suppose, for it actually — in one way or another — informs the Bible's entire understanding of history and of God's action in history. Indeed, it is not too much to say that the Bible — Old Testament and New alike — views the whole course of history in terms of a looking forward and a looking back, in terms of what God has done and what God will yet do, of former things and new, of that which is and that which is to be.

Since this is so, a study of the two ages will prove fruitful for one's understanding of Scripture as a whole, specifically of the relationship of promise to fulfillment and, therewith, of the relationship of Old Testament to New within the canon of Scripture. The Old Testament is a book before Christ, and thus a book out of the old age. It tells of God's dealings with Israel through the course of a long history. It is a very human history which knew success and failure, nobility and weakness, faith and unfaith, hope and bitter disappointment — in a word, a history which in itself might seem to have no exceptional significance.

Yet all through that history — from the call of Abraham, through the prophets, to the end of the

Old Testament period, and beyond — one sees a continual reaching out toward the future, toward a decisive action of God which would reverse the dreary course of this history, bring to pass the fulfillment of his promises and establish his kingly rule of justice and peace among men. But that hope found no realization in the Old Testament. The Old Testament is a history without conclusion, which down to its very last page still points ahead into the future toward the new age which God will bring.

The New Testament, in that it announces Jesus as the Christ (the Messiah), announces the inauguration of the new age. It declares that in Christ the kingdom of God is "at hand," and it summons men to citizenship and new life in that kingdom. It declares, moreover, that in the work of Christ, his death and resurrection, the new age has won its decisive victory over the powers of darkness and that, although the struggle still continues, it will go on to final victory at the Last Day, when "every knee should bow, . . . and every tongue confess that Jesus Christ is Lord, to the glory of God the Father." The New Testament thus views the history within which we live in terms of a cosmic struggle, and it summons the Christian to participate in that struggle. Again and again it lays before him the option: light or darkness, death or life, this present age or the age to come.

Probably most Christians are aware of this duality in the Biblical view of history, if only because their Bibles are divided into two parts, Old Testament and New, and because western culture has accommodated itself to the notion by dating events B.C. or A.D. But it is not so simple as that. Many profound questions remain. What is the nature of the old age and the new? What does it mean to live in one or the other? How do the two ages relate one to the other? If the victory of the new age has been won in Jesus Christ, how is it that the old age still continues? How is the Christian to live in this world, and face its problems, as a citizen of another world? What does it mean to be in this world, yet not of it? These are questions of profound theological and practical importance upon which many Christians wish guidance. They arise out of the Bible's own understanding of God's purpose in history, and they affect the Christian in his own self-understanding and in his daily living.

It is with questions such as these that Professor Halvorson seeks to deal. In doing so, he exhibits the marks of a gifted teacher. His study is firmly based in Scripture and remains true to the teachings of Scripture. In spite of its limited compass, it never descends into superficiality. Moreover, although it never condescends to the reader or "talks down" to him, it avoids that technical jargon which so often makes Biblical studies inaccessible to the average Christian. The style is simple, direct and brisk, and the presentation is larded with apt illustrations which serve the purpose illustrations are supposed to serve, namely, to make difficult points clear. What is more, the relevance of the Biblical teaching for the Christian as he lives in the world of today is never lost from view. It is a pleasure to commend this study. It will surely be of benefit to a host of Christians who wish guidance in understanding one of the central teachings of the Christian faith.

1

This Present Age

On Tuesday *Time* and *Newsweek* can be purchased at Miller's Drug Store. Both magazines report the events of the week throughout the world and attempt to provide an interpretation. The pages and the content of these magazines are rooted in this world and in this age.

Is it possible for a person to live in another age and in another world and at the same moment to live in this one? What is this other age? From the perspective of another age, what is the nature of this age? How do these two ages relate to each other? What will be their ultimate end and destiny?

As we seek to understand the mystery of this present age, Paul's epistle to the Romans will figure prominently in our discussions. In the latter part of Romans 5, the Apostle sets forth a significant

contrast between the first Adam and the second
Adam, who is Jesus Christ. Paul makes it very
clear that the theological significance of the first
Adam is that he initiated this present age. Sometimes it is called the old age. The first chapters of
Genesis tell us more about this old age than any
other portion of Scripture. Every significant contemporary study of Genesis ascribes Genesis 1 and
Genesis 2:1-3 to the priestly tradition of the Old
Testament. Chapters 2 and 3 are attributed to a
Yahwistic tradition which appears to have assumed
its written form first. Within the Temple at Jerusalem, Genesis 1 continued as a living oral tradition
for a longer period of time. Until the Temple at
Jerusalem fell in 587 B.C., there was no need for
this priestly tradition to assume written form. It
now appears that the Yahwistic tradition assumed
its form in the 10th century and the priestly tradition in the 6th century B.C. In both instances, very
old items have been brought within the covenant
community of Israel and have become a part of
the Scriptures. Within these Scriptures, a significant word is hidden for each generation. The Scriptures remain the same; but one generation may
see and hear something which an earlier generation
did not discover. On the other hand, our grand-
parents may have had better "spectacles" than we.
Nevertheless, there is something new about the
Word which is hidden within the Scriptures. These
opening chapters of Genesis are able to speak an

authoritative word for us today about the origin, nature, and destiny of man and about the age of which we are a part.

Man as Creature and Creator

The assumption of both traditions is that God made man from the dust of the earth. This is Scripture's way of affirming that man is a creature. Genesis 1 then proceeds to assert that God also made man in the image of God and that he is the one creature to whom God gave the entire creation with the injunction to have dominion over it, subdue it, and use it. According to Genesis 2 God breathed into the nostrils of man the breath of life; man then became a living person, who was to give a name to the other creatures. In Hebraic thought name and nature are one. If I know your name, I know some secret about you and have you under my thumb. In other words, to give a name assumes that you have dominion and power over the creature to whom you give the name. Both traditions assume that God made man from the dust of the earth. This is the language in terms of which Scripture asserts that you and I are creatures. Both traditions affirm in different ways that man is the one creature who has dominion over the entire creation, which the other creatures do not have. This uniqueness which God gives to man is his creative freedom. Man is also a kind of creator. In

Hebraic thought man is both creature and creator. Since man was not able to find an adequate companion among the other creatures, God created woman to be his helper, forming the first human community within Scripture.

Creative Freedom and Fellowship with God

The expressions for man's uniqueness in these chapters is the image of God. There is no explicit definition of the image. The emphasis is rather upon the responsibilities and opportunities of man which result from his creation in the image of God. The nature of the image is more implicit than explicit in these chapters and becomes more clear as the Hebraic faith unfolds in history. However, on the basis of some implicit assumptions, several characteristics of this image can be set forth. For example, what is the immediate context of the passage about the image in Genesis 1? The verses which follow are concerned with man's dominion over the whole creation. Man's uniqueness, more than anything else, is his creative freedom. A plant has no freedom. Clever horses and dogs have some freedom but it does not tempt them to an intense rebellion. Man is the only creature whom God singles out, giving him the entire creation. Consequently the things which man fashions with his fingers, hands, and mind have about them a certain majesty. One might call the things which man creates historical values. They tempt man to orient his existence around these historical values. The day will come when the misery of man will be rooted in the tricks which this creative freedom plays upon man.[1] These chapters also assume man's capacity for fellowship with God and his accountability to God. This is another characteristic of the image. Man is the only creature to whom God comes with the question: Where are you? In this encounter, man will use all the clever powers of his reason to deny his guilt. This indicates that man is something more than reason or body. With his whole self he is involved in temptation as well as in his relationship to God. This suggests a third assumption about the image of God.

Made for Community and Memory

Man is able to look at himself other than in a mirror. He can make himself his own object. He can not be contained within his own body. He must lose himself in the lives of other people. Among the animals whom he named, he found no adequate companion. So God created woman and began the first family. Because man transcends himself in his freedom, he is ultimately spirit or self rather than mind; at the same time man is a creature who is made for community. This is the third character- istic of the image in these chapters. In our encoun- ters with each other we become the person God wants us to become. This leads us to a fourth assumption about the image. Man lives in time; but another facet of his uniqueness is that time is in him. It assumes the form of memory. Tradition and memory are important factors in the Hebraic understanding of man. Man is able to reflect about his origin and contemplate his destiny. For this reason, man is the only creature who is able to write his own history. This is what the Yahwist is seeking to do in these chapters.[2]

Man's Ultimate Good

What does God intend man to become? In the tradition about the Garden of Eden, Scripture seeks to give us an authoritative answer. The garden contains two trees. The one is the tree of life; it has a sacramental function. When man eats from it, he will continue to live. Ultimately man is excluded from the garden so that he will not eat from this tree. The other one is the tree of the knowledge of good and evil. This tree is a constant reminder of man's freedom as a creature to be dependent upon God who made him and who is the source of his existence. In Hebraic thought, dependence is our ultimate good. It is, however, a dependence which embraces a respect for the will and purpose of God.

Concerning this tree of the knowledge of good and evil, there was a prohibition. To some ears, this prohibition has sounded primitive. The important factor is that there was a prohibition. It tells us that the freedom of man was not chaotic; it was a structured and ordered freedom. The Old Testament contains no formal concept of personality. Yet Walter Eichrodt has pointed out in his *Theology of the Old Testament* that all the ingredients of the concept are to be found within the Old Testament.[a] Furthermore, it is as personal will that God discloses himself to Israel. In his encounters with God, man becomes conscious of himself as a person. He is no longer submerged in the group. This means that he becomes a center of responsibility. Apart from this sense of responsibility, he remains subhuman. But man is made for responsibility and dependence. This is his most true and essential self. Another way to say this is to insist that man's freedom co-exists with his destiny. He is not intended to be a fish or a rooster. He is intended to be a man. Faith seeks to restore man to what God intended him to be. In this sense faith constitutes my existence. However, the faith that saves me must first of all slay me in my egocentricity. Only then can it become that dependence upon God and my fellowmen which is my true self. For the Hebraic and Christian understanding, faith means a radical dependence.

Man's Ultimate Evil

The tree of the knowledge of good and evil is also a reminder of man's freedom as a creature to rebel and assert his independence and autonomy. But rebellion initiates a false existence, and this is man's ultimate evil. It appears that the prohibition awakened in man the awareness of this possibility. This awareness is not sin; however, it does awaken in man fear and dread about its possibility. At the same time, there can be no real freedom without this counterpart, which is the possibility of un-limited freedom. Man is the one creature who can choose to separate himself from God forever.[4] In order to be a person, one must become a center of responsibility. The human tendency is to go over-board and declare one's own independence. Faith, on the other hand, is a radical dependence upon God who is the source of our existence. This is the basic structure of faith in the Hebraic and Chris-tian tradition. In the Garden of Eden, man lives in a tension of dependence and responsibility. This tradition is an authoritative portrait of what God intended man to be.

The Old Age Began in Rebellion

As we turn to Genesis 3, we meet a modified dualism. In the tradition, God does not directly create evil. Its origin is a mystery and for this reason, man is accountable and responsible for his evil. The temptation begins on the level of doubt. The whole man is involved with his hunger, lust, and possibility of pride. Earlier we asserted that the double nature of man in the Hebraic faith is creature and creator. This double nature is the occasion which makes sin possible. In Genesis 3, man is tempted to deny his creaturehood. He wants to become the pure creator. Only God is the pure creator. Sin then is ultimately rebellion against the source of our existence. A basic axiom of this believing community is that God really made us. As the Hebraic faith historically unfolds, it becomes clear that God wants us to be with him forever. Some day God will become the fulfillment of our existence. God then is the true end of our existence. In Genesis 3, Adam makes himself into an end of his own; but it is a false end. Man's uniqueness is a creative freedom which inevitably plays tricks on him. Man's misery is rooted in his dignity. It is because man possesses such remarkable creative freedom that he is able to tie himself up in such knots. It is this inevitable tendency of human nature which the author of Genesis seeks to illuminate.

A basic assumption of these first chapters of Genesis is that the creation is good. God saw what he had made and, behold, it was very good. What then is the old age? It is this world and what we have done with it in our rebellion. The old age is a quality of human existence. Adam is the organic head of the human race. In his rebellion, he initiated this present age. The theological significance of Adam, then, is that he initiated the old age.

History and the Old Age

Against this background, this question confronts us: What is the biblical understanding of history? In our discussion thus far, we have anticipated already an author and a book which constitutes a remarkable wrestling with this topic. It is *Faith and History* by Reinhold Niebuhr. This author contends that history is a mixture of nature on the one hand and our creative freedom on the other. There is the givenness of nature in creation. Man goes to work on it with his creative freedom and creates something new. It is the realm of history. This mixture of nature and freedom, however, is in movement. The past is constantly projecting itself into the present. It does so in two ways. Aspects of the past project themselves into the present with a revocable tentativeness. This means that there are things about our existence which can be changed. Other aspects of the past project themselves into the present with an irrevocable finality. This means that there are elements in our historical existence which are very stubborn and which cannot be changed. This grasp of the biblical understanding of history prompted Niebuhr to write this prayer which is familiar to many people:

> God grant me the serenity
> To accept the things I cannot change,
> The courage to change the things I can,
> And the wisdom to know the difference.

2

The Age to Come

Ancient man had made a rather elemental observation from which he drew an inevitable inference or conclusion. In the spring of the year, he would place a seed in the soil. At its proper time, it would germinate and then burst through the crust of the soil. If it was a cereal grain, it would ripen and eventually be harvested. After this came the cold death of winter. This happened with regularity each year. The inference was drawn that nature moves in a cycle. At this point we meet the further assumption that time and history are one with nature. The ancient Egyptians and Mesopotamians had a cyclic understanding of time and history.[1] This view leaves no place for novelty. That which will be is that which has been.

The Exodus Tradition and Israel's Sense of History

Against this background, the Exodus from Egypt represents a radical break in historical understanding. Jacob and his sons had come down into Egypt where their number increased considerably. Under Pharaoh they experienced oppression. Then God raised up Moses to lead them out of Egypt. Most scholars now accept 1290 B.C. as the date for the Exodus. The tradition about the Passover is presented in Exodus 12, and Exodus 14 contains the tradition about the liberation from Pharaoh's soldiers. At Sinai the law was given, a relationship of covenant was entered into, and the people were constituted as a nation. In these historical experiences of liberation and revelation, God disclosed himself and his purpose to the eyes of faith. At first Israel measured time from events such as the Exodus, the conquest of Canaan and its eventual settlement. When these events became related to each other in sequence, a linear view of time began to emerge. This does not mean that there is a straight line which runs through the Old Testament. Rather it means that from the Exodus, there is an orientation toward the future and a goal toward which God is leading history. According to Exodus 6, God had revealed himself as Lord in this event in particular. If he is really Lord, this means that the God of the Exodus created Israel and that Israel's future is also in his hands. It becomes the task of the prophets to make their understanding of this goal more explicit as the Hebraic faith unfolds in the experiences of history. The God of the Exodus is not one with nature; rather his purpose transcends nature, and this became an important factor in Israel's consciousness of history.

The Zion and Son of David Traditions

This Exodus tradition is adapted to many new situations throughout the Old Testament. After the conquest and settlement in Canaan and before the monarchy was established, the people understood themselves in terms of the Exodus and revelation at Sinai. Shechem in the north was an important center for this understanding of the covenant, and for this reason the ark was kept there. In the 10th century B.C., the united monarchy was established. When David made Jerusalem his capital, he moved the Ark of the Covenant to an elevation within the walls of this city which is called Zion. The people soon began to believe that this is where God had chosen to dwell among his people in a special way. Furthermore, the prophet Nathan made some very important promises to David about a future son who would rule on his throne for ever. After the death of Solomon in 922 B.C., the Northern Kingdom resumed its separate existence. It appears that the Exodus and Sinai election traditions continued to occupy a place of central importance for this

Northern Kingdom. The Zion and Son of David election traditions assumed a comparable significance for the Southern Kingdom of Judah.

Second Isaiah and the New Age

From time to time, this people understood themselves in new situations in terms of this Exodus tradition. A classic example of this is found in Isaiah 40–55. In 587 B.C., Nebuchadnezzar of Babylon had reduced Jerusalem and its Temple to rubble. This became the occasion for the second historical deportation of this people from Jerusalem to Babylon. The first deportation had taken place in 598 B.C. Throughout much of this century, these people lived in and around Babylon. In those days, there was among them a prophet who preached and taught them. We have his sermons in Isaiah 40–55. According to him this exile was not the end of God's purpose; through Cyrus of Persia, God would liberate these people so they could return to Jerusalem. However, in the thought of the prophet, this liberation would be another exodus. Furthermore, a new age would break in upon them when they returned to Jerusalem. The concept of a new exodus and a new age are at the heart and center of the theology which informs Isaiah 40–55. Toward the end of this 6th century, some people did return under the leadership of Zerubbabel. From 520 to 515 B.C., the Temple was built again back at Jerusalem. But the new age did not break in upon them. From then on, however, the concept of a new age or an age to come was never lost. After some years a new kind of literature, called apocalyptic, began to emerge. This literature had many characteristics, but its distinction between this age and the age to come is the most important item for our purpose.

The Exodus Tradition in the New Testament

Within the New Testament, the Exodus tradition is used again. One example is Paul's attempt to understand the new Israel as the people on whom and to whom a new age has come. Under Joshua the conquest of Canaan took place and its settlement by the 12 tribes. The 12 tribes became a name and a symbol for the old Israel. When our Lord began his ministry, one of the first things he did was to call 12 men to work together with him. By this act, he said to all men: "The old Israel defected from her calling. The old Israel did not become the holy nation which my Father in heaven sought to create. Now I, the Messiah, will create a new Israel." The Christian church is an historical expression of this new Israel. In his book *Paul and Rabbinic Judaism* W. D. Davies seeks for some key or unifying principle by which to interpret the details of Paul's epistles. He concludes that there is nothing more central to the thought and con-

viction of Paul in his letters than the distinction
between the two ages.[2] We shall illustrate this sug-
gestion with reference to 1 Corinthians 10:1-13,
an important Pauline text for our purpose.

In this Corinthian passage, Paul takes us back to
the Exodus and the wilderness journey under Moses.
First there is reference to the event at the Red Sea.
Together with the Passover, the liberation of the
people from Pharaoh at the sea constitutes the medium of deliverance. The tradition is found in
Exodus 14. Paul says some things in 1 Corinthians
10 about Moses that can be said technically only
about Christ. In Exodus 14, the people were not
baptized actually into Moses. For Paul, Moses is
the prototype of Christ. The next event is the food
and the drink which the Lord provided for these
people in the wilderness journey. In Exodus 16,
manna is provided and in Exodus 17, there is the
rock which yielded drink. The Lord met his people
with food and drink, and this constituted the medium of nourishment. Before the Word of God
became flesh and dwelt among us, Paul is saying
that Christ is the dynamic who formed Israel and
propelled Israel forward to the fullness of time.

The Wilderness Tradition in the New Testament

Paul elaborates the third historical reference with
considerable detail. It involved the historical wilderness journey itself. Four experiences are singled out.

The first refers to the incident of the golden calf
in Exodus 32. This was an initial act of rebellion
on the part of Aaron and the people. Then he turns
to the end of the 40-year journey in the plains of
Moab. Numbers 25 relates what happened at Baal-
Peor when the men of Israel began to forsake their
families and take Moabite women. This kind of
syncretism would have dissolved the purpose which
was initiated in the Exodus and at Sinai. For this
reason, there was an intensity about the judgment
which came upon the people. Then Paul takes us
back to Kadesh where the people spent more time
than at any other place. In Numbers 21, the people
murmured against the Lord who took them out of
Egypt. By now life had become even more difficult,
and they longed to return to Egypt. The judgment
came upon them in the form of serpents. The
tradition tells about a bronze serpent lifted up to
become the means by which the people would be
healed. The final incident centered about Korah and
his 250 men. In Numbers 16, they became dissat-
isfied with the authoritarian leadership of Moses
and Aaron. The people were still in the area of
Kadesh. This was another act of rebellion and there
is a mystery about the judgment that came upon
the people.

What is the intention of Paul in making these
many references to the Exodus and the wilderness
journey? Paul seeks to understand human existence
right now in terms of the historical wilderness jour-

ney. Life then and now is fraught with acts of
rebellion against him who is the source of our
existence. Within Scripture, the wilderness is used
frequently as a symbol for this present age. The
Exodus, then, is to the Hebraic faith of the old
Israel what the cross and resurrection are to the
faith of the new Israel. In this Corinthian passage
Paul asserts that the end of the ages has already
broken in upon us. In his epistles, Paul does not
always use the term *age to come* or *new age,* but
the substance of the concept is there. In this passage, Paul tells the people of his day that they, too,
have passed through the sea. For Paul, baptism is
the act of incorporation into the new age. There
is also the medium of nourishment. The risen Lord
continues to meet his people in the wilderness with
food and drink as they kneel at the altar to receive
his body and blood. In the fullness of time, the
Word of God became flesh. Paul is convinced that
this Word of God participates in the salient events
of the Exodus. This Word was the dynamic which
formed Israel and impelled Israel forward to the
fullness of time. For Paul there was a wholeness to
revelation that undergirded his use and understanding of the Old Testament.

The Two Ages as the Key for Romans

In his classic commentary on Romans, Anders
Nygren contends that the distinction between the

ages is the unifying factor in Paul's epistle. In Romans 5:12-21, Paul sets forth a series of contrasts between the first Adam and the second Adam, who is Jesus Christ. Nygren contends that this is the heart of the epistle where Paul sets forth the theological basis for his distinction.[3] In the perspective of Paul, the significance of Adam is that he initiated the old age. He is the organic head of the human race; but beyond this, he is an ordinary man. By way of contrast, Paul contends that no ordinary man could have initiated the new age. At Mount Sinai, the Ten Commandments became a historical expression of the will and law of God. Before the time of Moses, sin was not an explicit defiance of the law since it had not yet received particular historical expression. However, this does not mean that the old age began with Moses. In his rebellion, Adam initiated the old age which continues as a quality of human existence, through the stubborn persistence of rebellion like that at the time of Moses. Adam's uniqueness is that he is the organic head of the human race with whom the old age began. On the other hand, Jesus Christ is the second Adam, who initiated the new age to which we now belong through faith. The law as well as death are among the dynamics of the old age. We never quite outgrow our initial reaction to the law. I say to my daughter: "Rebecca, do not touch those papers on my desk." I have barely spoken the command and her little hand reaches

out after them. The law activates and intensifies
rebellion in each of us. It is an aspect of the power
of sin and together with sin gives the human experience of death the sting and enmity which it has
in this present age. In contrast to law and death,
the dynamic of the new age is grace. In the events
of Christ and Pentecost, this grace has been secured.
It is experienced by every believer as pardon and
power. Paul's name for grace in Romans is frequently the righteousness of faith. While the law
may increase the tendency to sin, this grace will
always abound much more.

Another logical question with which to wrestle
is this: How and on what basis did the new age
enter this world? One of the remarkable Jewish
theologians in this second half of our century is
Abraham Heschel. His special concern is the conviction of the prophets about God, man and history.
Heschel articulates their convictions in terms of
the pathos of God. This doctrine means that Israel's
God is involved and participates in human history
in a manner which was not appropriate to a deity
in the Greek world. In Hellenistic thought, God
did not repent and suffer. While the prophets con-
tend that God can not be coerced and manipulated,
nevertheless the Holy One of Israel is responsive to
the attitude of people. The pathos of God expresses
itself constantly in terms of wrath and mercy. This
raises the question: How do God's wrath and mercy
relate to each other? In the theology of the prophets

at this point, it can be said that God overcomes God. God's wrath which expresses itself in acts of judgment is overcome by his mercy which expresses itself in promises and acts of deliverance.[4]

The Moral Content of History and Its Basis

What further ought to be said about the basis and reality of the new age in this world? In Romans 3:21-26, Paul establishes the theological ground for the new age. Already in the preceding chapters, Paul has explicated a very basic presupposition of the Hebraic and Christian faith. He has made it clear that with God there is no distinction of person. Furthermore, God never abrogates the distinction between historical good and historical evil. For this reason, history has a moral content. For the Christian faith as well as the Hebraic faith, there is nothing more real than God's wrath and God's mercy.[5] This gives vitality to the Hebraic and Christian ethic. In order to forgive, God must take upon and into himself our rebellion. Paul contends that God did this as he put forward Christ Jesus as an expiation by his blood. The term *expiation* could be translated *mercy-seat*. The language and thought takes us back to Leviticus 16 and the institution concerning the day of the atonement. Once a year the high priest entered the holy of holies and sprinkled blood on the mercy-seat in order to expiate his own sins and then the sins of the people. In

terms of the devotional life, the sacrifices of the old
Israel had some value. They did mediate blessings.
However, in terms of the actual procurement of
forgiveness they had no value. In a climactic way
and with finality, this procurement took place at
the cross and in the resurrection. Here God took
upon himself our rebellion. In anticipation of this
event, the sacrifices of the old Israel could mediate
blessings.

The Reality of the New Age

In this world, my situation is one of existential
estrangement. I know deep within what God has
intended me to be. But my life in this world con-
tradicts this norm. I have estranged myself from
what God would have me be. The good news of
the Gospel is that Christ Jesus was not overcome
by this existential estrangement in which he par-
ticipated as true man. At the cross and in the resurrection, he conquered this existential estrangement.
Unless our Lord had appeared in personal life within existence and subjected himself to the conditions
of existence, the new age would be only a longing
and an expectation. It would not be the reality in
space and time which it is in the biblical proclamation. I know of no author who has formulated this
better than Paul Tillich in *Existence and Christ.*[6]
The new creation in Christ Jesus is the organizing
principle in the thought of this author. Tillich is

convinced that the new creation in Christ is the most relevant formulation of the answer to the anxiety and frustration of modern man. He insists that unless Christ Jesus were true man, he would not have entered fully into our situation and that unless Christ Jesus were true God, he would not have triumphed fully over this estrangement for us. Only when this receives central emphasis is the Gospel taught and preached in its fullness and richness.

3

The Dynamic of the New Age

The prophets of the Old Testament had many convictions. One of them centered in the ultimate end toward which God was leading history. Isaiah and Micah in the 8th century B.C. articulated this belief in terms of Mount Zion, the elevation within Jerusalem on which the Temple was built. In the latter days, they contended, Zion will be exalted and become the great center of the world. Through the authority of his word, the Lord will judge among the nations of the world who will come to Zion. By means of the word which goes forth from Zion, the Lord will settle disputes among the nations. Paradise restored was another portrait in terms of which they communicated their understanding of the end of history. For our present purpose, it is important to notice that this end would be here on earth after the contradictions of sin have been removed by acts of judgment. The ultimate end will consist of a people here on earth over whom a unique son of David will rule in a new age. The prophets also shared the conviction that the creation is good. In fact it is so good that the covenant community will remain forever here on earth.

The Time Between the Testaments

The events narrated in the Old Testament close at approximately 400 B.C. and were followed by the intertestamental period. Toward the end of the 4th century B.C., the Persian empire yielded to the rule of Alexander from Macedonia. When Alexander died at a young age, his empire broke up into several units. Syria and Palestine became a part of the Seleucid Kingdom with its capital at Antioch. Some of these kings persecuted the people of Jerusalem and Judah with an intensity which had few parallels in Israel's history. Antiochus Epiphanes, who ruled about 170 B.C., remains the most famous symbol of this ruthlessness. No wonder the scribes and teachers of Israel concluded that the government of this world was in the control of the devil. In those days much apocalyptic literature was written, though very little became a part of the Old Testament canon. This literature had many characteristics; but for our purpose, its distinct dualism is most important. It tended to make a separation between this world, which was evil and in the

control of the devil, and the age to come, which
was a reality beyond space and time. The emphasis
of this apocalyptic literature was quite different
from the classical prophets. This evil age will be
brought to a sudden end by a transcendent son of
man who will appear on the clouds of heaven to
initiate the age to come.

The Quality of Existence in the New Age

Our Lord was born into a world that thought in
terms of this apocalyptic dualism. Jesus began his
ministry with the affirmation that this age to come
was now already at hand. His miracles were signs
that pointed to this new age. The Apostle Paul was
very much a part of his own day when he employed
the distinction between the ages. He was convinced
that the battle of the ages had taken place. On
Good Friday, it appeared as if the old age would
triumph. Then on Easter and Pentecost, the reality
of the new age broke in upon us. Paul also shared
the conviction of the prophets that the creation is
good and that the old age had authentic values even
though it could become demonic. Furthermore,
there is something about this world that makes it
impossible for even God to enter directly in all of
his majesty. He has come always as a hidden God.
The technical name in our theology for the hidden-
ness of God is the theology of the cross. The new
creation in this world is hidden but it is real. Bap-

tism is God's act of incorporation into the new age. The entire New Testament is concerned about the quality of our existence in this new age as believers. Inasmuch as we are both a creature and a creator, we need a standard or a guide to supplement and complement our existence as individuals. Because our creative freedom is so great, this norm must be ultimate. In many places, the New Testament sets forth this norm in terms of love. It is not just the kind of love which likes a person but the kind of love which is willing to empty itself for another. Matthew 5, 6 and 7, Romans 12, 1 Corinthians 13 and 1 John 4 articulate the structure of our existence within the new creation in a more definitive way than most other passages. Reinhold Niebuhr refers to the exhortation and commands which confront the believer in these passages as impossible possibilities.[1] Because our creative freedom is so great and this norm so ultimate, the life of the believer is one of unending striving. We are the kind of creature and creator who can find meaning only in yearning and striving. A premature fulfillment will thwart all meaning. The New Testament addresses this norm to man in his individual existence, and for that reason the ethic of the New Testament is one of discipleship.

Baptism as Act of Incorporation

Only for purposes of thought can a distinction be made between the act of incorporation and the dynamic which Paul sometimes calls the righteousness of faith. First we shall turn to Romans 6:1-11 where the act of incorporation is set forth. In this passage, Paul uses the metaphor of death and burial. In baptism we die and are buried with Christ into death. However, Christ was raised from the dead and so we, too, are to walk in newness of life. In our baptism and as believers, we have been incorporated already into the final goal of history.

At the same time, the old age has its own dynamic. Consequently the old has a strange effect upon us. Many of the things we create have real values and even a majesty about them. They tempt us to orient our existence around these historical values. Because our creative freedom is so great, we are constantly tempted to idolatry. Man becomes enslaved to the things he has made with his fingers and mind and ultimately he becomes enslaved to his own self. In the event of the cross and resurrection, the old age was defeated but not annihilated.

Baptism is the act of incorporation into the new age. The risen Lord will settle for nothing less than the commitment of our whole self to this new age. The old age has been defeated and our relationship to it is to be one of death. In Christ, every believer has been made alive. As Romans 6 continues, Paul tells us that the old age seeks to enslave; but the new age sets us free. Does this mean that the new age abstracts us and lifts us out of the old age? Paul is very emphatic that the new age sets us free from our enslavement to this world of historical existence so that we can struggle with the old age. In *The Bondage of the Will,* Luther employs this famous illustration: Man is like a horse which must have a driver. Both God and the devil seek to drive.[2] The new age seeks to set us free so that we can enjoy the creation, which is good, as God intended it to be used.

The same illustration of man as a horse in need of a driver is used by the Danish Christian thinker Søren Kierkegaard. He tells about a rich man who brought from abroad to Denmark an excellent team of horses. They had been trained originally by a royal coachman. The rich man did not know how to drive this team. Soon they became lazy like any ordinary team of horses with all sorts of quirks and bad habits. The owner, who was no coachman, simply held the reins and let the horses run as they wished. So the rich owner decided to procure for the team of horses the royal coachman who originally had trained them. He came and soon the horses began to carry their heads proudly, their eyes were fiery and their pace was beautiful. Man is like a horse; he needs a driver. The author concludes his illustration with this basic lesson and exhortation: "We have been governed, trained, and educated according to man's conception of what it is to be a man. You see what has come from that — we lack spiritual stature. . . . There was a time when it pleased the Deity Himself, if I may say so, to be

the coachman, and He drove the horses according
to a coachman's conception of what driving is." [3]
If it were not for the dynamic of the new age, this
world, which seeks to enslave us, would enthrone
itself.

Grace as Pardon, Power and Presence

What do we mean by the dynamic of the new
age? In Romans 1:16–17, Paul speaks of it as the
righteousness of faith. Elsewhere he calls it grace.
For Paul as well as others in the New Testament,
this grace is both pardon and power. Suppose I
have been a pastor in your congregation for four-
teen years. I am slow of speech, the young people
make me nervous, and I would rather withdraw
from people and read a theological book. In spite
of this, things have gone quite well and the congregation has grown. The church board has decided
to call a young graduate from the seminary to be
an assistant pastor. He is a fluent and imaginative
speaker, loves the young, and enjoys mixing with
people. After some months, the inevitable happens.
A sizeable group within the congregation who in
the past had responded to my efforts now begin to
rally around him. This poses the question: How will
I respond to this situation? I am a human being
and I can respond only as a human being. Inasmuch
as I work in the church, I know how I ought to
react. I ought to live above it. But how will I respond deep within? I will be out to get this young

man. I shall have to be very clever and pull a veneer of piety over what I say and do. In this situation I represent the established order, and he is a new emergent who threatens me.

The old age began with an act of rebellion and it continues into the present with my rebellion. My independence is a false autonomy and for this reason, I am easily threatened. This prompts me to ask: Is there any kind of power that could penetrate deep within, melt my pride and make me so strong in the inner person that I could adjust to that which threatens me? The answer of the New Testament is grace. It is both pardon and power. It can penetrate deep within and make a person so strong that he can yield to the threatening new emergents and adjust to them. This grace has the outward appearance of weakness; yet, it is able to do that which not even the atomic bomb can do. It gives me a radical self-acceptance that liberates me. When we take grace seriously as the dynamic of the new creation, we realize that grace is also a presence, namely, the Holy Spirit. Paul affirms in Romans 5:5 that the love of God has been poured into our hearts through the Holy Spirit which has been given to us.

Before we leave the above illustration, we want to return for a moment to the young pastor who threatened me. At the right moment and without telling a single person, he began to change and build me up among the congregation. This began to give me a sense of security. I need to be able to do a few things well. This sense of security is sometimes called common grace. The Christian faith never belittles common grace; rather it sees all the little securities of life as gifts from God's good creation. More than I realize, it is through the experiences of common grace that I come to know the grace of Christ.

The Death and Life of Jesus Made Manifest

The central dynamic of the new age is Jesus Christ. One of the great texts on this topic is in 2 Corinthians 4. In this passage Paul reviews the contradictory experiences of his ministry. These are some of the contrasts: afflicted but not crushed, perplexed but not driven to despair, persecuted but not forsaken, struck down but not destroyed. Then he makes these two affirmations: We carry about in our bodies the death of Jesus; the life of Jesus is manifested in our mortal flesh. He concludes with this confession: "So death is at work in us, but life in you."

At the edge of a city where I served as a pastor was a large prison. One winter we studied 2 Corinthians in the congregation. For some thirty years our Sunday school superintendent had been a guard at the prison. I shall always remember the evening we took up Chapter 4. I had called attention to Acts 14 and its account of Paul and Barnabas on their first missionary journey. In Asia Minor they visited Iconium, Lystra and Derbe. At Lystra they were stoned and Paul was dragged out of the city. I had called attention to Acts 16 with its story of Paul and Silas on their second journey. This time they got up into Philippi of Macedonia. There they were dragged into the market place, their garments were torn off, they were beaten with rods, and then placed in prison with their feet in stocks. I had called attention also to 2 Corinthians 11 where Paul tells us that on five different occasions he received 40 lashes less one.

About this time our Sunday school superintendent spoke up. He told us about a man in his crew down at the prison. One day he had taken off his shirt and shown them his back. He had deserted his family in Canada. The people of the community found him, then bound and beat him. He had lashes imbedded in the flesh of his back. Suppose you met the Apostle Paul some day and asked him: "Paul, do you believe this gospel you preach, about a kingdom and a Christ who is risen and alive forevermore?" How do you think that he would answer? I think he would take off his shirt and show you his back. In Paul's case it was literally true that he carried about in his body the death of Jesus. As people witnessed his life, they said to themselves: "There must be something to this gospel Paul preaches. Look at what he has endured." In other words, the life of Jesus was manifested in his flesh.

No wonder he could say to others: "So death is at work in us, but life in you." Many came to faith as they witnessed his life and heard the proclamation. For Paul this proclamation was not simply a handing on of something that had to be preserved; it was an event that summoned the dead and the godless to life.

Agents for Change in History

How do I carry about the death of Jesus now and how is his life manifest in my body? You and I are members of many communities. Some are more intimate and private; others are more public. It is always in our encounters with each other that we become the person God wants us to be. We are made for community. These communities give a sense of fulfillment to our existence; at the same time they are also a frustration. I make them a frustration because I want to dominate others within the community. Nothing is more disruptive of community than pride. There is no point at which I suffer more than when others will not yield to my dominion and I cannot have my own way. The dynamic of the new age will make me strong enough to begin to die to self and thereby truly to live. As I die to self I can more easily include the other person in my life, and as the other person dies to self he can more fully include me in his life. The risen Lord becomes manifest in the quality of life he seeks to create within our communities.

In an earlier chapter we raised the question about the Hebraic and Christian understanding of history. We suggested that history is a mixture of nature given in creation and of our creative freedom. But this mixture is in motion. The past is constantly projecting itself into the present. On the one hand, it does so with revocable tentativeness: some things can be changed. On the other hand, some aspects of the past project themselves into the present with irrevocable finality: there are factors in our existence which can not be changed. This is the basis for a realistic attitude, but we dare not become determinists. There is much about life which can be changed and made new. What is the basis for change, and where do we receive strength to activate change? The grace which is the dynamic of the new age is the basis of indeterminate renewals and creativity. While aspects of the old age are stubborn, the entire orientation of the new age is toward the future and change. This raises the next inevitable question as to how change unfolds in history.

4

How the Ages Relate to Each Other

In the Garden of Eden man lived in a tension between responsibility and dependence. This dependence embraced a respect for the will and purpose of God.

Another name for this will and purpose is the divine command. Some of the Psalms in the Old Testament express clearly this divine command or *torah*. Psalms 19 and 119 are good examples. An able theologian of our day has suggested that these words could well be the reflection of a believer in any century of time: "Yet my response to this will that stands over me and confronts me as an other is to greet it with an inward Yes, with joy. For I am created for this will. I perceive that it desires only life, my life. The law of my own being is such that I can only have true life by reposing in God's love, in utter trust and self-surrender." [1] This is the response of a creature who is dependent on God.

But Adam was not content to remain a creature and creator. He wanted to become like God. He wanted to become the pure creator. This led to rebellion. Now he responded to the divine command and heard it in a totally different way. It had the sound of law and met him as an enemy that both activated and intensified sin. This is the way Jeremiah understood the law given at Sinai when he spoke the promise of a new covenant. According to Jeremiah 31:31–34, there will be need for another mighty act of God which will restore the divine command. This happened at the cross, in the resurrection, and at Pentecost. In these events of fulfillment, the divine command became rooted in an indicative act.

In 2 Corinthians 5, Paul's name for this action is the new creation. It is against this background that we must understand a certain kind of discourse Paul employed in his epistles. Recent biblical studies have given considerable attention to this form of exhortation. We find this form especially in Deuteronomy and the table of duties in the Pauline epistles.[2] It says in effect: "Become what you already are and will be in Christ Jesus." The entire New Testament is concerned with the structure of our existence in the new age. The uniqueness of the divine command now is that it is rooted in an indicative act. Reinhold Niebuhr refers to the divine command met in passages such as Matthew 5, 6 and 7, Romans 12, 1 Corinthians 13, and 1 John 4 as impossible possibilities.[3] These ultimate demands are spoken to man in his individual or private existence. How then do these demands relate to the old age or his public existence? Are they directly applicable in a simple way?

As One Who Lives in Two Ages

We want to pose the question as to how the two ages relate to each other in history. For purposes of illustration, we shall use two examples. In our first example, we shall assume that you are on a church board and that your pastor is gone. You have been asked to speak at the Sunday morning service. You select Matthew 5:38–40 as a basis for your meditation because it has intrigued you for some time. Here our Lord speaks some ultimate demands. The most familiar is this one: "Do not resist one who is evil. But if any one strikes you on the right cheek, turn to him the other also." You have made the point emphatically that if we are Christians, we will strive to take this demand seriously. You have challenged the congregation to live in the new age.

On Sunday afternoon your neighbor and his wife come to see you. They are expecting their first child. As never before they have wanted to be Christians. He works in a shoe factory which has no insurance or pension program. The union has been patient in negotiations; but when management completely rejected even modest proposals, a strike was voted. Your neighbor has been asked by the union to participate in the strike on the following Tuesday. He really listened to your message. Now he asks whether he can participate as a Christian.

In the second example, it is your turn to conduct a Bible study in your congregation. You select a passage from Romans 12 because it is your favorite. Romans 12:9–16 contains these exhortations: "Let love be genuine; hate what is evil, hold fast to what is good; love one another with brotherly affection ... Bless those who persecute you ... Live in harmony with one another." You have made it clear that Paul is talking about the new age here in Romans 12. This is what life is to be like in the new age. Among the people in your class is a man who has a small business in your city. He is a responsible man and has a son at the seminary preparing to become a pastor. This man has three men of Italian background, two men of Polish background and one man from Puerto Rico working in his business. He needs one more man and has advertised for someone who could qualify. A black man has applied and the owner of the business has discovered that he is a very responsible person. He now informs the other men who are working for him, and they threaten to walk out if he hires the black man. Because of the nature of the work and the time it takes to train them, this would ruin his business. At the same time, he feels that it is his duty to respect the integrity of every person in our society. He wants to take seriously the divine command of the new age. He asks you: "As one who dwells in two ages, what am I to do in this situation?"

The Norm for Man's Private Existence

Most people never ask how these two ages are related to each other. The question has been raised only in scattered moments throughout the long history of the church. When men and women take their relationship to Christ and their participation in the new age seriously, then the problem of how the two ages relate to each other becomes real; it causes believers much anguish of heart. How does God work in the old age now? How does God create justice in the rough and tumble of economic and political life? How does the believer who is not abstracted from the old age participate in these activities? Where does he say no and on what basis does he participate?

We shall attempt to make a number of distinctions. Our point of departure has been made already with the Apostle Paul. He takes seriously the Hebraic teaching about the double nature of man. Man is a creature and also a creator. Man's uniqueness in comparison to other creatures is his creative freedom. In terms of economic and political organizations, man has been able to create over the centuries new forms within which his vitalities function. During these last decades technological progress has been almost incredible. All of this is rooted in the apparently unbounded freedom of man. For this reason, man needs an ultimate norm or standard to guide and supplement his existence. The norm of the new age is love, not the love which likes only certain people; but the kind of love which is willing to empty itself for others and even die to self. These ultimate demands are made on every believer in the new age. They comprise an ethic of discipleship. Consequently, the demands are spoken to man in his individual or private existence.

The Norm for Man's Public Existence

It is in the old age that we meet man in his collective and public existence. This embraces the rough and tumble of economic and political life. In this area of existence, man also needs a norm or guide to supplement his existence. It will have to be a more proximate norm. Is there any place within Scripture where a man of God spoke to a collective or public group, such as a nation, and articulated such a norm? This was the task of the Old Testament prophets. They spelled out the norm in terms of justice and righteousness. Where does the prophet get the norm of justice? It is rooted

in his understanding of the goal toward which God
is leading history. At times the prophet pictures this
end of history in terms of a people over whom the
son of David will rule in righteousness. This vision
of the end possesses and animates the prophet in the
present. The norm is also rooted in the past. The
God of the Exodus had delivered their fathers from
oppression in Egypt and told them, "You shall not
oppress a stranger . . . for you were strangers in the
land of Egypt." It is the nature of justice to calculate. It says something like this to the other party:
"If you do this, I shall do that." Love, on the other
hand, does not calculate; it is willing to empty
itself. Because justice is arrived at through compromise, it is inevitable that the justice of today
will become the injustice of tomorrow unless it is
informed by something more ultimate. We dare
not deify the structures of the moment and make
them too rigid. They must remain open to change
so that the norm of justice may be implemented.

Augustine's Question

This same problem emerged in the days of Augustine. By the time he became a responsible leader
of the church in North Africa, Christianity had
been the official religion of the Roman Empire for
several decades. Even before Constantine affirmed
the privileges which were to be given to Christianity in 313, people had spoken about eternal Rome

for centuries. Now some thought that Rome would be buttressed by the gospel and really stand as a political structure for ever. Then in 410 the Goths invaded Italy and pillaged Rome. This event became a portent of the future. Many began to ask why this judgment came on the eternal city. For the previous century, many had been converted to Christianity and had forsaken the old gods of Rome. Some believed that these deities had awakened now and had begun to inflict this judgment. Others concluded that when Rome began to fall, nothing of Christianity remained, because for them the political structure and the Christian faith were essentially one. In this situation, Augustine equated the new age with the city of God and contended that Rome belonged to the old age, that it was a city of this world. In order to understand the real reason why Rome fell, he argued that one had to distinguish between these two cities. The fall of Rome could not be explained in terms of converts to the city of God, nor did this political event effect the validity of the Christian faith.[4]

How God Ruled for Luther

The same problem posed itself again in the 16th century. Whenever there is a profound application of the word of God to the human situation, some such distinction must be made. Luther equated the new age with the kingdom or realm of God's right hand. Here, Luther contended, God rules with his word. In the realm on his left hand, God rules through secular authority. An attempt to relate the word of God to the political and economic events of his day compelled Luther to make this distinction. He is dependent on the earlier distinction of Augustine between the two cities. The historical situation and intention of Luther is set forth carefully by George Forell in his book *Faith Active in Love*. Forell suggests that Luther became so preoccupied with the Pope as the religious aspect and the Turks as the political aspect of the anti-Christ, that this drove him to an apocalyptic dualism.[5]

Another excellent discussion is in Heinrich Bornkamm's monograph, *Luther's Doctrine of the Two Kingdoms*. Bornkamm contends that the issue is this: "How God continues to keep alive a world which has fallen prey to death, after the new aeon in Christ has already been inaugurated in its midst and has become a reality in the life of Christians through the Holy Spirit." [6] A profound social ethic must make a distinction between these two realms or kingdoms; but it is easy to go beyond this and to separate them. Then the realm on the left becomes independent and autonomous. This can lead only to irresponsibility on the part of the church. This temptation has confronted historic Lutheranism. The heroic stand of Eivind Berggrav and most of the Norwegian church during the second World War was a noble example to the contrary.[7]

A Modern Prophet in Detroit

As this 20th century opened, industry began to emerge as a vast center of power. In many places men and women who labored in large plants became victims of this tyrant. It was a kind of feudalism. Samuel Gompers was one of the early leaders who championed the rights of labor. In 1915 a young man became pastor of a congregation in Detroit, Michigan. Most of the men in his small parish worked for Henry Ford. The pastor would call at homes where the man of the house had become ill while working in the Ford plant. At that time the automobile industry could not have cared less about conditions that prevailed among its unemployed. The young pastor was Reinhold Niebuhr.[8] He began to ask himself how the ultimate demands of love could be related to the problems of this city. The leaders in many churches at this time assumed that if Henry Ford were converted, the problem would be solved. Niebuhr observed that this would be no better than to tell an alcoholic that if he were converted, he then could drink all the whiskey he desired. The reason is that economic power also intoxicates and is even stronger than whiskey. Once again a distinction had to be made between moral man on the one hand and immoral society on the other. In the realm of the collective and public which is the old age, one had to be a realist. Industry had become a center of power. Niebuhr contended that labor must become another center of power. God is at work in these organismic factors of society. Justice will be achieved as one center becomes balanced off against another. In 1932 Niebuhr's great classic on this topic appeared in print with the title *Moral Man and Immoral Society*.[9]

We have already obliquely raised our next question: How does justice elbow its way out into society? How is God at work in human history today to create justice? At this point the prophets of the Old Testament are realistic and relevant. God is at work seeking to create justice through two regulative principles. The one is liberty. Its classic expression is the commandment: Thou shalt not steal. This commandment assumes the right of a man to own property and to develop it. This right creates initiative and responsibility. However, the Old Testament prophets observed how easy it was for man to go overboard at this point. The man who had one farm wanted another. In those days, some sought to add field to field and house to house until there was no more room in the land. In every century, there has been a deeply rooted tendency for society to stratify itself. As men have attempted to secure their own existence, the wealthy have become wealthier and the poor have become poorer. For this reason, there has been a need for equality as another regulative principle. The prophets in their passion for justice frequently identified themselves with this regulative principle.

In our day, these regulative principles have become vast organismic factors and centers of power. The irony of history is that now within a single center of power, forces are contending with each other. This prompted Reinhold Niebuhr to write an editorial in 1961 entitled "The New Feudalism." He calls attention to and reflects on the tremendous changes within the International Brotherhood of Teamsters. The problem which labor and industry at one time posed in relationship to each other is now a comparable problem within organized labor between some leaders and the union itself.[10] The church can thwart or stimulate justice to the extent that it recognizes that God is at work in history right now in the midst of these organismic factors.

Why Justice Needs Love

This realistic conviction about the way God works to create justice in the old age is predicated on a distinction between the ages. This need to distinguish poses the danger and temptation to go a step further and to separate the two realms. The delicate balance of power and its resultant justice in one decade may easily become a source of oppression if left to itself. Justice is the norm of the old age in the thought of the prophets and it is the nature of justice to calculate. It is necessary for justice to say to other members of society: If you do this, I shall do that. Because compromise is a factor in justice, it is easy for justice in one decade to become injustice in another. Justice is not a static norm. It must constantly be informed by love. Love is the norm of the new age. While it is not relevant in a simple and direct way to the rough and tumble of economic activity, it is ultimately desperately relevant. This kind of love constantly judges justice and inspires it to greater works. If Christianity is to retain its integrity, it must not soften the biblical emphasis upon the ultimacy of love.

In other words, the two ages do penetrate and are intended by God to penetrate each other. I may be a somewhat different person in my public life than I am in my private life. But I remain a single person and live in both ages at the one and same time. A good example is politics. Politics is the art of getting along with others in the old age. There never has been such a thing as Christian politics; but the hope for our society is that there will continue to be Christians and humanists with a concern for others in politics. Their days of active labor will not be easy. The new age does not abstract us from the old age. It sets us free so that we can struggle with the old age and seek to restore its authentic values. Men and women engaged in the struggle for justice must also remember that their faith will not automatically supply the cor-

rect answer to the complicated and technical problems of the old age. If the believer should forget
this, he will be tempted to an offensive arrogance
and pride. At the same time, earnest Christians will
continue to exert an influence far beyond their
numerical figure.

5

The Destiny of the Ages

The dualism of the two ages that emerged in the centuries before Christ became a part of the abundant apocalyptic literature. In the Old Testament it is represented by the book of Daniel. There is more of it in the Apocrypha. However, it dominates a third collection of writings known as the Pseudepigrapha. During the first century of this era, people thought in terms of this dualism. It is also found in the New Testament. In the thought of Paul, the old age was initiated by the first Adam. It embraced this creation, which is good, and as such it has authentic values. For this reason, the believer's task is to rejoice in his existence and to strive to restore the values of this present age. No greater significance could be attached to historical existence than the event of the incarnation. This is a consistent emphasis of the New Testament. Nevertheless, the old age is this world and what we have done with it in our rebellion. It is a quality of human existence. It is not demonic; although it can become demonic.[1]

God Enters as the Hidden One

The end of the old age has come and a new age has broken in upon us in the events of Christ and Pentecost. God was in Christ and dwelt among us in the historical Jesus. He initiated the new age. However, the new age has continued to remain a hidden reality in this world. This emphasis is sometimes called a theology of the cross. If the new age were to become a deified institution in this world, it would be a theology of glory. Baptism is the act of incorporation, and we live now in the age to come by faith. Faith is a radical dependence. Consequently, to assert that we live by faith really means that the new age grasps and possesses us. For our present purpose it is important to remember that in this world the new age is a hidden reality. This is the only way true deity can enter this world.[2] But what is hidden must some day be unveiled. The new age has already broken in upon us but it is not complete. Some day its destiny will be disclosed. Until the end comes, the two ages will continue to clash. This is the theme of Revelation with which the New Testament closes and to which now we shall return.

The History Which Produced the Book

The Book of Revelation is apocalyptic literature and possesses its historical characteristics. In contrast to intertestamental literature, the event of Christ has affected this book. To sort out the kinds of literature is basic for all interpretation. It is also important to know the historical situation out of which it emerged and to which it was written. This is especially important for the Book of Revelation.[3]

At one point, Roman history is like American history. It divides itself into two distinct units. The watershed of American history is the Civil War. Even if one knows the history of this country very well up to the Civil War, this does not mean that one could possibly understand our contemporary institutions.

The earlier period of Roman history is known as the Republic. It began with a simple and thrifty city state which developed gradually into a great power. The center of power was the Roman senate. As the city state expanded, an army was necessary. As the army became larger, its generals became more powerful. These generals threatened the senate and posed a challenge for leadership. This came to a climax when Julius Caesar was murdered in the Roman senate. It was now evident that a vast reorganization of the government was necessary. An emperor was needed to control the generals. The watershed in Roman history was the rule of Octavian from 27 B.C. to A.D. 14. He became the first Emperor or Augustus. He let the senate remain but it no longer possessed the substance of power, only the appearance of power. The government he initiated is called the principate and its period of history is known as the empire.

The relationship between this government and the primitive church was quite good at first. Emperor Claudius ordered a persecution in the year 49; but only the Jews were involved. It was still easy to be a Christian. About the year 55 or as late as 57, Paul wrote his letter to the Romans and in Chapter 13 expressed gratitude for the Roman government and the peace it sustained throughout the world. However, clouds began to gather when Nero ascended the throne, and the first explosion came in 64. At that time it was much easier to be a Jew than a Christian. In the course of time, Nero died and the church thanked God. Again, there were some years of peace. Toward the end of the first century, Domitian revived all the persecutions of Nero.

There is a sense in which man creates his own political organizations. This is not to deny the fact that such organizations also assume a momentum that carries individuals along with them. Government is a historical value and also a relative value. Whenever a government lifts itself up above criticism, it becomes an absolute, but a false absolute.

This is the way the demonic enters history. It happened in the days of Nero and again under Domitian. This is the historical background of Revelation, written about A.D. 90 to believers who lived under this tense political situation.[4]

The Structure of the Book

In Chapters 2 and 3, the risen Lord through the medium of his servant speaks seven messages to seven historical congregations in Asia Minor. In Chapters 4 through 7, the Lord is seated on his throne and holds in his right hand a scroll sealed with seven seals which no one is able to open. Only the Lamb who stands near the throne is able to open this scroll. As these seven seals are opened, the first distinct cycle of the book is unfolded. It is a vivid picture of the two ages as they clash during the interim which began with the first advent of our Lord and will continue until his second advent when he returns to complete his work. This interim in which we now live is called the three-and-a-half years, the 42 months or the 1,260 days at other places in the book. Chapters 8 and 9 contain another cycle of seven trumpets that are blown. In Chapters 15 and 16, seven bowls of wrath are emptied out. Each of these units or cycles ends on the same note. It is a climactic rebellion against God; at the end of Chapter 16 it is called the Battle of Armageddon.

What is the word of the Lord hidden in these chapters for the church today? The emphasis here is that man is a creature and that God has singled man out from the other creatures for unique responsibilities. Only man is to have dominion over the whole creation. Man's uniqueness is his creative freedom. The double nature of man in Hebraic thought is creature and creator. Because man is also creator, he produces progress in this world. It takes place in the area of historical values. The things we create with our hands and minds have about them a certain majesty. They impress us and tempt us to orient our existence around these relative values. Our creative freedom plays tricks on us. As we make absolutes out of these historical values, they become false absolutes. The more progress that takes place, the more we are tempted to this kind of idolatry and rebellion. Some day the rebellion of the old age will become climactic. How will God deal with this climactic rebellion? He will take hold of history as a ripe fig tree and shake it. These are the eschatological judgments. Each of the cycles or units in the Book of Revelation ends on this note. However, this is not the end of God's purpose. God acts beyond these judgments and creates a new heaven and a new earth.

The Inevitable Tensions

The Book of Revelation contains a kind of literature somewhat foreign to our day. It emerged at a moment in history when the church feared that it would be overcome by oppression and opposition. Consequently, its attitude toward history is so realistic that it is almost cynical. In scattered moments of history this book has again become alive for believers. While Bishop Hanns Lilje of Hanover, Germany, was imprisoned by the Nazi government during the Second World War, he began to write a commentary on this book. These words set forth Lilje's conviction that this book illuminated his experience: "When the course of history becomes more and more stormy, when volcanic upheavals lay bare the depths of existence, Christendom may be more inclined to listen to the message of the last book of the Bible. As the prophets perceived the coming of the supreme Lord in all the fluctuations of contemporary history, and as Augustine in the midst of the devastations caused by the fall of Rome and the appearance of new historical institutions again inquired into God's plan for the world, so amid the upheavals of the present time we too seek to discover the lines which God has laid down for us to follow in his plan. But the church of Jesus Christ must know that she can never distill such a plan out of her own speculations on the philosophy of history; one thing only she does possess: the world of prophecy. The prophet knows the secret of history because he knows its end." [5] There is also a profound optimism in this last book of the Bible. It is rooted in the risen Lord whose future is not fully disclosed. As a Lamb and as a Lion of the tribe of Judah, he goes forth conquering and to conquer. The historic and biblical Christ is the dynamic of the new age. On the one hand, this book reflects realism, and on the other hand it witnesses to optimism. These two points of view contradict each other. Even in a somewhat normal period of history, my life as a believer is lived in a tension between the ages. The norm of the new age is ultimate; baptism has begun a life of endless striving. But in the midst of striving I can appropriate the promise of grace without feeling that I am a phony. In this book the tension between the ages becomes so great that they clash with each other. At times the old age appears to triumph. However, in the end it is the new age that becomes unveiled and victorious. This is the assurance the book seeks to bring to believers living under intense persecution.

A Key Chapter

One has not come to grips with the Book of Revelation until he has wrestled with Chapter 12 and Chapters 13 and 17, which are predicated upon it. Then in Chapters 19 and 20, the climactic judgments break forth once again. Chapter 12 divides itself into three distinct units. In the first paragraph we meet a woman clothed with the sun and with the moon under her feet. The many details in this book were understood by the people at the end of the first century, but we are too far removed from the social, economic and political life of that day to understand them completely. It is poor interpretation to read mysterious meanings into these details. The Scriptures may even lose some of their authority as a result.

The woman in Chapter 12 is with child and gives birth to a son who is to rule the nations with a rod of iron. Near the woman stands a red dragon with seven heads and ten horns, eager to devour the child, but the son is caught up to the throne of God and protected. The woman is the old Israel from whom Christ is born according to the flesh. The dragon is identified as that ancient serpent, the devil. When our Lord was only an infant, the principalities and powers of this age were represented by Herod and the struggle or encounter began with the demonic.

In the second paragraph of Chapter 12 we read of a war that takes place in heaven between Michael and the dragon. Michael conquers and casts the dragon out of heaven to the earth. Michael represents the new age, and the dragon the old age. This is a good apocalyptic picture of the atonement. The war between Michael and the dragon is symbolic of the battle of the ages. The old age is defeated but not annihilated. In the last paragraph of Chapter 12 the woman appears again. She is in the wilderness and the dragon attacks her but can not conquer her. The woman now is the new Israel. In a sense, it is the same woman for there is a continuity between the old and the new Israel; but there is also a discontinuity. The woman is in the wilderness, a good biblical symbol for this world. The dragon attacks but can not conquer.[6]

The Realities to Which Symbols Point

In Chapter 13, we read of a beast who rises out of the sea. We meet this same beast again in Chapter 17. Like the dragon, the beast has seven heads and ten horns. The beast is the agent of the dragon in this world. The author identifies the beast with many oblique historical and political references. One of the seven heads of the beast received a mortal wound but now it has been healed. In Revelation 17:7–9, the beast is identified as one who "was, is not, and is to ascend from the bottomless pit," which is the abode of the demonic.

Again we are told that the seven heads of the beast represent seven hills. In those days of political tension, the author had to use language which disguised the political reality that threatened the church. This beast appeared in the person of Nero. Nero was and then he died so that he is not. Now in the person of Domitian, he is ascending once again from the bottomless pit. Government is a historical value; but when it lifts itself above criticism, it can become demonic. This beast has appeared on the historical horizon from time to time. No wonder the faithful church in Germany saw the beast's identity in Hitler. Biblical realism compels us to say that the beast will appear again.

Chapter 17 describes another woman who is seated on the seven heads of the beast and whose name is Babylon. In complete contrast to the woman of Chapter 12, this woman is a harlot. She represents the many other ancient Roman activities, cultural and economic, related intricately to the political state. Babylon is the city of this world and as such is more inclusive than the beast with seven heads and ten horns. At the end of Chapter 13, we read of another beast that has two horns like a lamb but a beast that speaks like the dragon. If the first beast that rose out of the sea represents the political aspects, then this other beast that rose out of the earth represents the religious aspect of the antichrist. It had its concrete expression in pagan Roman religion. The climactic rebellion at the end of time will be created by the beast in its political and religious aspect. As such this beast is a symbol of the stubborn persistence of rebellion in human history.[7]

In the beast with seven heads and the harlot who is seated on its seven heads, which are seven hills, as well as in the second beast which also was called the false prophet, the old age has risen in defiance against him who is the source of our existence. How then will God deal with history? He will take hold of history like a ripe fig tree and shake it. These cataclysmic judgments are pictured for us in Chapters 19 and 20. Already in Chapter 18, the harlot, Babylon, has fallen and the merchants of the earth weep while the people of God rejoice. Then at the end of Chapter 19, the beast with seven heads and the false prophet are cast into the lake of fire. At the end of Chapter 20, the dragon is cast into the lake of fire. The dualism which the Scriptures assume is modified; it is not ultimate. The earlier part of Chapter 19 presents a picture of a bride who is busy preparing her wedding dress made of fine linen; the fine linen consists of the righteous deeds of the saints. This bride is the new Israel and she is awaiting her marriage with the Lamb at the marriage supper. As the church is engaged in real acts of love, she is preparing her wedding dress.

Two Perspectives on the Political State

In Chapters 21 and 22 of Revelation, the bride appears again as the new Jerusalem. This bride is the new age which the risen Lord is creating now; but in this world, the bride is hidden. Some day she will be unveiled as the new Jerusalem.

Before we turn to the new Jerusalem in Chapter 21, one more observation must be made about the beast with seven heads. The identity of this beast was clearly a demonic political state at the close of the first century. The beast is pictured vividly in Chapter 13 and again in Chapter 17 of Revelation. In Chapter 13 of Romans Paul is discussing this same political state. This was at an earlier date, perhaps as early as 55. Paul is grateful to God for the blessing this political state has brought to all people. Through the peace which it has sustained opportunities have come to the church. The ages do not always clash against one another with the same intensity. Paul sees real values in the old age and is anxious that the people of God participate in its life and activity. This is the only way faith can authenticate itself. Toward the end of the first century, however, the attitude of the primitive church toward the political state was completely different. In the second century after the apostles were disappointed in their expectation that the end was very imminent, the church began to understand itself in a different way. A strong emphasis on the sacramental presence and structure of the church emerged.[8]

The New Age Unveiled

Throughout the history of Christendom, the new age has been hidden. Some day it will be unveiled. Then it will become the new Jerusalem which descends out of heaven as a bride adorned for her husband, who is the Lamb. This new Jerusalem is pictured as a vast city with 12 gates named for the tribes of Israel. The walls of this city are built on 12 massive foundation stones. On each stone is the name of one of the apostles. Each of these stones is adorned with other stones to attract attention to the names of the apostles. The 12 tribes are a symbol of the old Israel; the 12 apostles are a symbol of the new Israel. The author's intention is to remind us that the foundation of Jerusalem is the apostolic witness and testimony. Some day, the new age will be unveiled. Then it will become the new Jerusalem. All the contradictions of sin will be removed. This is the content of our destiny.

Courage to Change

Two great confessions in the New Testament call for our attention: "Beloved, we are God's children now; it does not yet appear what we shall be, but we know that when he appears we shall be like him, for we shall see him as he is. . . . One thing I do, forgetting what lies behind and straining forward to what lies ahead, I press on toward the goal for the prize of the upward call of God in Christ Jesus." 1 John 3:2 and Philippians 3:13–14. In Christ Jesus we have our identity as children of God. As believers, we are open toward the future rather than slavishly attached to the past. Our calling is a high one. We press on toward the ultimate goal and destiny to which we are summoned.

This means that as believers we must be open to radical change that will involve discontinuity with the past. The future toward which we strive has a content. However, in the midst of change, the con-

tinuity with the past will be strong. As the past
projects itself into the present, some aspects can
not easily be changed. As individuals and as a society we can absorb only so much change at a time.
At this point, the new Israel of which we are a part
has a special responsibility. The gospel also contains
tradition rooted in the past. But it must never be
understood as something only to be preserved. Its
proclamation always seeks to become an event that
summons the dead and godless to life. The new age
is able to set us free from those elements in the old
age that seek to enslave us and make us too defen-
sive to change. Consequently one can measure the
real strength of a person or a community by its
ability to absorb constructive change. Our great
need and a part of our calling in every community
of which we are a part is to be a people who have
the courage for constructive change.

Love and Justice

This has been a study in the eschatological nature
of the people of God. It is best understood against
the background of a classical view which domi-
nated Christian thought for many centuries. This
classical view is rooted partly in static Greek dualism. Basic to this classical view is a distinction
between this fallen world of nature and a second
level which is above and which is the domain of
created supernatural realities. In this perspective,

salvation is a matter of escaping one by one from this lower level of time and matter into the higher level of heaven. In contrast to this view, there is the Biblical emphasis on the end as *eschaton* which has entered this world of horizontal time. In this world, the new creation is hidden and at the same time present as a dynamic for social change.

In the Book of Revelation as well as in history, the political order, the economic order, and the religious order are closely related, and in different periods of history one or the other order will seek to dominate as much as possible. Whenever some relative order pretends to be absolute, it becomes demonic. This order will bear for the moment the primary responsibility for injustice. In tension with these institutions of the old age is the new creation which is present first as a promise and since the first advent of Christ Jesus as fulfillment. The structure of life in this new creation is expressed in terms of the ultimate norm of love. The form which love takes in this old age is justice. It is the nature of justice to calculate. It is not as ultimate as love. For this reason, justice needs to be informed by love. Love will sit in judgment on justice and inspire it to greater works. The very presence of the new age in this world of horizontal time must impel the people of God to struggle for justice, and as such they will participate in the creation of a healthier society.

Notes

CHAPTER 1

1. Niebuhr, Reinhold, *The Nature and Destiny of Man* (New York: Charles Scribner's Sons, 1941), Vol. I. A basic presupposition in the thought of Niebuhr is the conviction that the Hebraic and Christian faith illuminate the historical drama. But it must be the authentic faith; otherwise there will be a false illumination. For this reason, he takes seriously biblical studies as well as the history of doctrine. This discussion of Genesis 1-3 is indebted to Niebuhr's biblical analysis and exposition.

2. Childs, Brevard S., *Memory and Tradition in Israel* (Naperville: Alec R. Allenson, Inc., 1962).

3. Eichrodt, Walter, *Theology of the Old Testament*, trans. J. A. Baker (Philadelphia: Westminster Press, 1961), Vol. II, pp. 120ff.

4. Heinecken, Martin J., *The Moment Before God* (Philadelphia: Muhlenberg Press, 1956), pp. 150ff. This is an introduction to the thought of Søren Kierkegaard. The pages indicated discuss S.K.'s *Concept of Dread*.

CHAPTER 2

1. Wright, G. Ernest, *The Old Testament Against Its Environment* (London: SCM Press, 1950), pp. 9ff.

2. Davies, W. D., *Paul and Rabbinic Judaism* (London: S.P.C.K., 1935), pp. 223ff.

3. Nygren, Anders, *Commentary on Romans*, trans. Carl C. Rasmussen (Philadelphia: Muhlenberg Press, 1949), pp. 213ff.

4. Heschel, Abraham J., *The Prophets* (New York: Harper & Row, 1962), p. 229. Moltmann, Jürgen, *Theology of Hope* (New York: Harper & Row, 1967), p. 131.

5. Forde, Gerhard O., *The Law-Gospel Debate* (Minneapolis: Augsburg, 1969). One of the major themes in this work centers about the dialectic between God's wrath and His love. Forde proposes to understand this dialectic in terms of the reality of Christ's death on the one hand and the reality and newness of His resurrection on the other hand. The proper formulation is important to propel the believer to participate in Christ's death and resurrection rather than to abstract and absolve him from such existential participation. See pp. 74–75 and 92–93.

6. Tillich, Paul, *Existence and Christ* (Chicago: The University of Chicago Press, 1957). This is Vol. II in his Systematic Theology, pp. 98 and 114–16.

CHAPTER 3

1. Niebuhr, Reinhold, *An Interpretation of Christian Ethics* (New York: Harper & Brothers, 1935), pp. 118ff.

2. Luther, Martin, *The Bondage of the Will*, trans. J. I.

Packer and O. R. Johnston (London: James Clarke & Co., 1957), p. 103.

3. Kierkegaard, S., *For Self-Examination,* trans. Edna and Howard Hong (Minneapolis: Augsburg Publishing House, 1940), p. 102.

CHAPTER 4

1. Althaus, Paul, *The Divine Command,* trans. Franklin Sherman (Philadelphia: Fortress Press, 1966), p. 10.

2. Von Rad, Gerhard, "Ancient Word and Living Word" *Interpretation* Vol. XV (January 1961), pp. 3ff.

3. Niebuhr, Reinhold, *An Interpretation of Christian Ethics* (New York: Harper & Brothers, 1935), pp. 118ff.

4. Cochrane, Charles N., *Christianity and Classical Culture* (London: Oxford University Press, 1944), pp. 509–513.

5. Forell, George W., *Faith Active in Love* (Minneapolis: Augsburg Publishing House, 1954).

6. Bornkamm, Heinrich, *Luther's Doctrine of the Two Kingdoms,* trans. Karl H. Hertz (Philadelphia: Fortress Press, 1966), p. 33. This book also contains an excellent chapter on the relation between Augustine and Luther on this topic. For a primary source, see Luther's "The Sermon on the Mount" in the American Edition of *Luther's Works.* Vol. 21, pp. 105ff. This volume is edited by J. Pelikan and published by Concordia Publishing House.

7. Berggrav, Eivind, *Man and State,* trans. George Aus (Philadelphia: Muhlenberg Press, 1951).

8. Niebuhr, Reinhold, *Leaves from the Notebook of a Tamed Cynic* (New York: Willett, Clark and Colby, 1929).

This volume is his own autobiographical account of this experience in the form of a diary.

9. Niebuhr, Reinhold, *Moral Man and Immoral Society* (New York: Charles Scribner's Sons, 1932). It is apparent to the readers that this writer has been influenced greatly by the books and articles of this modern prophet who has labored on the American scene.

10. Niebuhr, Reinhold, "The New Feudalism" *The New Leader*, Vol. XLIV (August 28, 1961), pp. 13ff.

CHAPTER 5

1. Mowinckel, S., *He That Cometh*, trans. G. W. Anderson (Nashville: Abingdon Press, 1956), p. 261ff.

2. Kierkegaard, S., *Philosophical Fragments*, trans. David F. Swenson (Princeton: Princeton University Press, 1946), pp. 20–21.

3. Rowley, H. H., *The Relevance of Apocalyptic* (New York: Harper & Brothers, 1943). Russell, D. S., *Between the Testaments* (Philadelphia: Muhlenberg Press, 1960).

4. Dawson, Christopher, *The Formation of Christendom* (New York: Sheed & Ward, 1967), pp. 67ff. Bruce, F. F., *The Spreading Flame* (Grand Rapids: Wm. B. Eerdmans Publishing Co., 1958), pp. 161ff.

5. Lilje, Hanns, *The Last Book of the Bible*, trans. Olive Wyon (Philadelphia: Muhlenberg Press, 1957), p. 14.

6. Rissi, Mathias, "The Kerygma of the Revelation of John" *Interpretation*, Vol. XXII (January 1968), pp. 3ff. Welch, Adam C., *Visions of the End* (London: James Clarke

& Co., 1922), pp. 211ff. Hendriksen, W., *More Than Conquerors* (Grand Rapids: Baker Book House, 1940).

7. Niebuhr, Reinhold, *Faith and History* (New York: Charles Scribner's Sons, 1951), pp. 214ff.

8. Moltmann, Jürgen, *Theology of Hope* (New York: Harper & Row, 1967), pp. 154ff. Tillich, Paul, *A History of Christian Thought* ed. Carl E. Braaten (New York: Harper & Row, 1968), pp. 40–41.